Y0-BSV-582

to

_____

from

_____

It is good to embrace a hope.

— OVID

The Silver Book of
HOPE

PUBLICATIONS INTERNATIONAL, LTD.

Photo credits: Front cover: **Darrell Gulin/Tony Stone Images** (center); **Sacco Productions Limited/Chicago** (background).

FPG International: Color Box; Richard Gaul; Michael Goodman; Peter Gridley; Richard Price; Telegraph Colour Library; Christoph Wilhelm; **International Stock**: Bob Firth; Ron Sanford; **SuperStock**.

Louis Weber, C.E.O.
Publications International, Ltd.
7373 North Cicero Ave.
Lincolnwood, Illinois 60646

Permission is never granted for commercial purposes.

Manufactured in China.

8 7 6 5 4 3 2 1

ISBN: 0-7853-3738-5

Original inspirations written by:

Elaine Creasman is a writer and poet. She writes for a variety of inspirational magazines including *Guideposts* and *Decision*.

Lain Chroust Ehmann is a columnist for the *San Jose Mercury News*. She writes on inspirational topics for numerous publications.

Margaret Anne Huffman is an award-winning writer and journalist. She has authored and contributed to numerous titles including *Simple Wisdom, Graces,* and *Family Celebrations.*

Marie Jones is a published writer of fiction and non-fiction stories as well as the author of several screenplays.

Other quotations compiled by Cathy Ann Tell.

The University of Chicago Press: lines from *The Odes of Pindar,* translated by Richmond Lattimore, copyright 1947 by The University of Chicago.

*Hope blooms
like a beautiful rose
amidst the thorns of life.*

*Hope is the lone flower
blooming in times of life's desert.*

Hope steadies the faltering soul.

Hope is like the sun,
which, as we journey towards it,
casts the shadow of our burden behind us.

— SAMUEL SMILES

Hope is the glue
that binds the pieces of a shattered dream,
making it shiny and new and whole again.

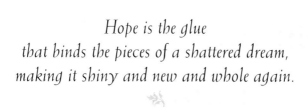

We have this hope,
a sure and steadfast anchor of the soul,
a hope that enters the inner shrine
behind the curtain.

— HEBREWS 6:19

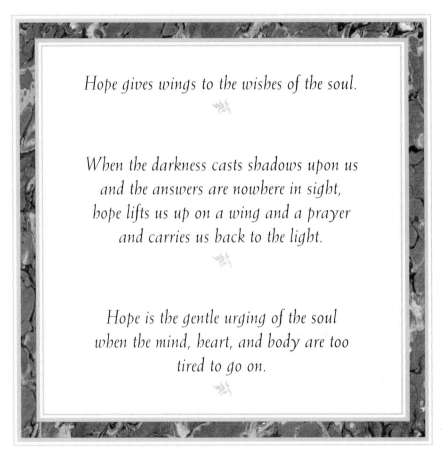

Hope gives wings to the wishes of the soul.

*When the darkness casts shadows upon us
and the answers are nowhere in sight,
hope lifts us up on a wing and a prayer
and carries us back to the light.*

*Hope is the gentle urging of the soul
when the mind, heart, and body are too
tired to go on.*

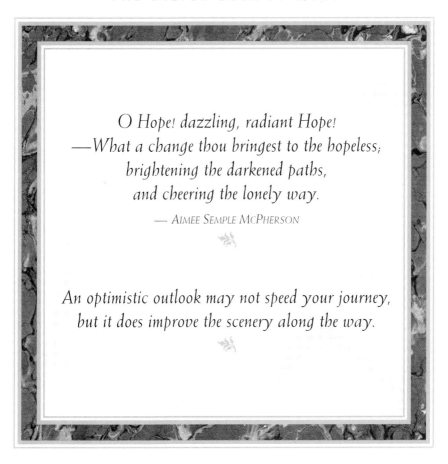

O Hope! dazzling, radiant Hope!
—What a change thou bringest to the hopeless;
brightening the darkened paths,
and cheering the lonely way.

— *AIMEE SEMPLE MCPHERSON*

*An optimistic outlook may not speed your journey,
but it does improve the scenery along the way.*

If you do not hope,
you will not find what is beyond your hopes.

— St. Clement of Alexandria

*Hopeful eyes perceive the light
where other eyes see only night.*

*Hope is about believing
with a humble heart
that tomorrow can be different.
It's about knowing
that light will come
to chase away this darkness.*

There is no priceless jewel
or precious gem
that can outshine hope.

Ah, Hope!
what would life be,
stripped of thy encouraging smiles,
that teach us to look
behind the dark clouds of to-day,
for the golden beams that
are to gild the morrow.

— SUSANNA MOODIE

Without seeming rhyme or reason,
hope allays the soul's worries
with the certainty of hummingbirds,
who know precisely the day to fly south.

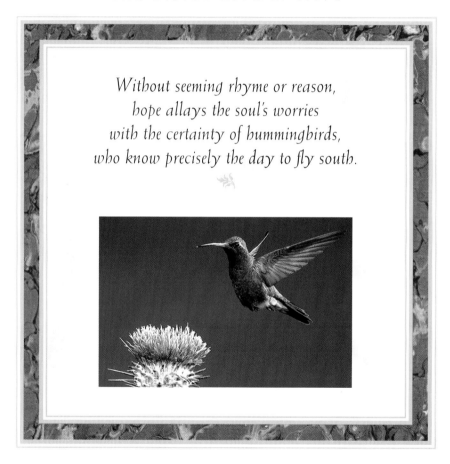

When all of our earthly hopes
seem like castles in the sand,
we can hold to this—
heaven is our home,
and we are but sojourners here.

Hope is a waking dream.

— *ARISTOTLE*

Today,
I long
to make a difference—
to pass along
peace and joy
and somehow
resurrect hope
in weary hearts.

Hope, like dawn, touches the darkness with light,
opening us to the new day coming.

Hope is the soul's faithful friend,
holding its hand through the night
and saying, "There will be a glorious dawn."

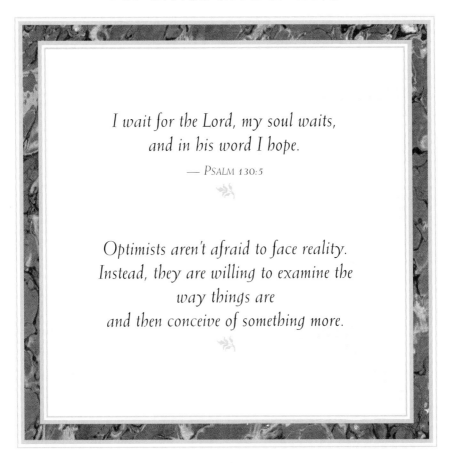

I wait for the Lord, my soul waits,
and in his word I hope.

— PSALM 130:5

Optimists aren't afraid to face reality.
Instead, they are willing to examine the
way things are
and then conceive of something more.

It is easy to be hopeful in the day
when you can see the things you wish on.

— ZORA NEALE HURSTON

Hope melts the frost from the tiniest leaf,
allowing it to grow stronger
in the healing light of the sun.

A despairing heart mumbles,
"God is doing nothing."
A hopeful heart inquires,
"God, what are you going to do next?"
and looks forward to celebrating
God's awesome ingenuity.

Hope springs eternal in the human breast;
Man never Is, but always To be blest.

— ALEXANDER POPE

Hope shouldn't mean holding
only one dream;
open yourself to any possibility
that the future may offer.
We may think we know what
we want for our lives,
but God answers prayers
in his own way.

Each new stage draws me like bee to flower.
There, hope prompts me to unfold the petals
and dine on the nectar of my future.

Hope, like the glimmering taper's light,
Adorns and cheers our way;
And still, as darker grows the night,
Emits a brighter ray.

— OLIVER GOLDSMITH

Hope whispers to the weary heart,
"Hold on."

Hope comes as a ray of sun
amidst the cold, dark rain,
moving us into the light
where love can heal our pain.

Hope springs eternal
like a well from deep inside us,
moving us into the light
where love can guide us.

*Love and the hope of it are not
things one can learn;
they are a part of life's heritage.*

— MARIA MONTESSORI

*Hope knows
on the other side of pain
is joy;
on the other side of injustice
is peace.*

Hope does not disappoint us,
because God's love has been poured
into our hearts.

— ROMANS 5:5

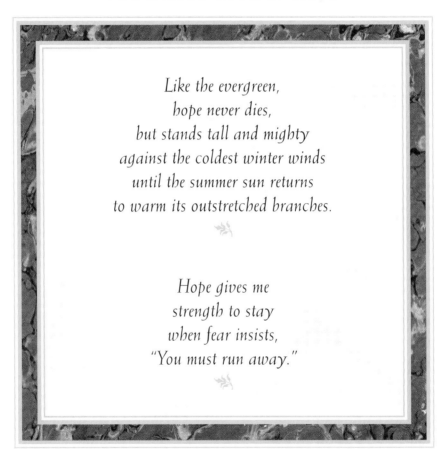

Like the evergreen,
hope never dies,
but stands tall and mighty
against the coldest winter winds
until the summer sun returns
to warm its outstretched branches.

Hope gives me
strength to stay
when fear insists,
"You must run away."

*What can be hoped for
which is not believed?*

— ST. AUGUSTINE OF HIPPO

*Offering hope to others
through a loving word,
a thoughtful act,
or a simple smile
is the surest way
to lift your own spirit.*

Hope costs nothing.

— COLETTE

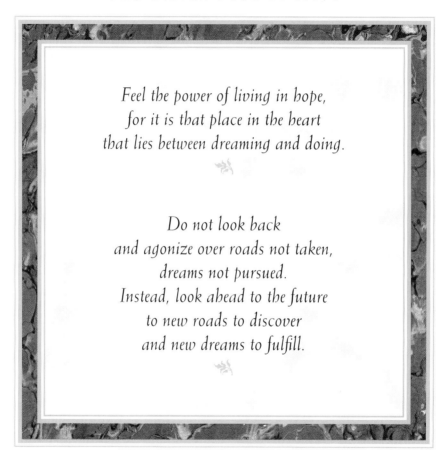

Feel the power of living in hope,
for it is that place in the heart
that lies between dreaming and doing.

Do not look back
and agonize over roads not taken,
dreams not pursued.
Instead, look ahead to the future
to new roads to discover
and new dreams to fulfill.

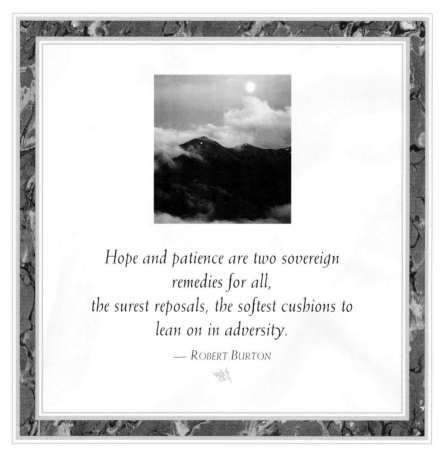

Hope and patience are two sovereign
remedies for all,
the surest reposals, the softest cushions to
lean on in adversity.

— ROBERT BURTON

To live in hope means to expect that our
longings will be fulfilled.
When we hold that image of
fulfillment constantly,
we cannot help but notice all the ways
in which our lives are blessed.

Who bids me hope, and in that charming word
Has peace and transport to my soul restor'd.

— GEORGE LYTTLETON

What does it take to live a life of hope?
Nothing more than a willing heart.

Hopeful people have a peace about them,
a way of looking at everything that happens
as an opportunity for growth and happiness.
Their lives are not any easier than anyone else's;
it's their attitude that sets them apart.

Rejoice in hope,
be patient in suffering,
persevere in prayer.

— ROMANS 12:12

When your dreams seem unreachable,
trust that the future will
lighten your burdens,
smooth your path,
and urge you on to a brighter tomorrow.

Hope is the most pleasing
Passion of the Soul.

— ELIZA HAYWOOD

Hope opens our hearts
And lessens our woes.
It fights against strife
And vanquishes foes.
It can be as small as a smile
Or as long as the day.
It's a gift that grows larger
When you give it away.

Hope acts as a power tool
that breaks the chains of our captivity
and shatters the bonds of negativity.

Hope is the parent of faith.

— CYRUS AUGUSTUS BARTOL

Scattered by a loving hand,
signs of hope are as close as
crocuses
unfurling in the snow.

There be no potion so powerful,
no pill so amazing,
no promised reward so alluring
as the certain belief
that something good can happen tomorrow.

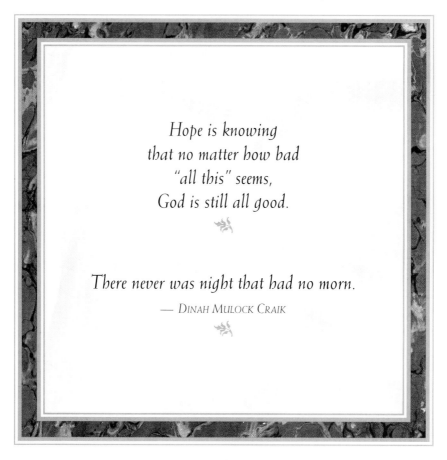

Hope is knowing
that no matter how bad
"all this" seems,
God is still all good.

There never was night that had no morn.

— DINAH MULOCK CRAIK

Hope is never wasted.
It is always beneficial,
if only to clarify
what we want from life.

For in hope we were saved.
Now hope that is seen is not hope.
For who hopes for what is seen?
But if we hope for what we do not see,
we wait for it with patience.

— ROMANS 8:24–25

*Hope is the joyful liberation of the heart
from the darkest prison of despair.*

Seated on an outcropping of rock
high above the snowbound valley,
my eye is drawn to the evergreen,
and hope stirs within my breast.

It is hope which maintains
most of mankind.

— SOPHOCLES

Heart of mine,
sing boldly
the songs of hope
to chase away
the gloom.

The difference
between a person who quits
and one who keeps on
through storm and struggle
is a hopeful heart.

Even now I am full of hope,
but the end lies in God.

— *PINDAR*

Hopeful eyes look upward,
penetrating the thick blanket of clouds
to the clear blue skies beyond.

Hope says,
"No matter how many times
I fall,
I will stand
and start again."
For a person of hope
is not one who never falls,
but one who picks herself up
one more time than she falls.

Comforting words for a weary heart,
a balm that soothes the soul,
hope is a healing medicine
that makes us strong and whole.

People of hope
ascend hills
and mountains
others have declared,
"Impossible."

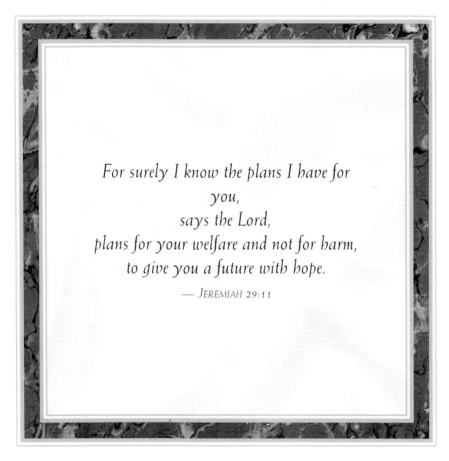

For surely I know the plans I have for
you,
says the Lord,
plans for your welfare and not for harm,
to give you a future with hope.

— JEREMIAH 29:11

Hope is not immune to reality
but transcendent of it.
Hope lifts us up to higher ground,
where we can see the bigger picture,
the wider vista,
the far horizon.

Hope knows
that in the midst
of feeling all alone,
God is still with me.

Hope swells my sail.

— JAMES MONTGOMERY

*To have hope is to stand
amidst life's coldest, darkest storm
and see the glorious rainbow
forming on the horizon.*

*Hope is the guiding lantern
that leads us out of the darkness of the forest
and into the safety of the clearing.*

*If it were not for hopes,
the heart would break.*

— THOMAS FULLER

Hope keeps the heart whole.

— ANTONY BREWER

Instead of searching for hope,
seek God.
Hope will be your constant companion
when you do.